DESIGN YOUR FUTURE

CAREERS

IN THE STUDIO

Shantel Gobin

Rourke

T0011432

Before Reading: *Building Background Knowledge and Vocabulary*

Building background knowledge can help children process new information and build upon what they already know. Before reading a book, it is important to tap into what children already know about the topic. This will help them develop their vocabulary and increase their reading comprehension.

Questions and Activities to Build Background Knowledge:

1. Look at the front cover of the book and read the title. What do you think this book will be about?
2. What do you already know about this topic?
3. Take a book walk and skim the pages. Look at the table of contents, photographs, captions, and bold words. Did these text features give you any information or predictions about what you will read in this book?

Vocabulary: *Vocabulary Is Key to Reading Comprehension*

Use the following directions to prompt a conversation about each word.

*   Read the vocabulary words.
*   What comes to mind when you see each word?
*   What do you think each word means?

Vocabulary Words:

*   apprenticeship
*   collaborate
*   freelancers
*   gig
*   industry
*   portfolio

During Reading: *Reading for Meaning and Understanding*

To achieve deep comprehension of a book, children are encouraged to use close reading strategies. During reading, it is important to have children stop and make connections. These connections result in deeper analysis and understanding of a book.

Close Reading a Text

During reading, have children stop and talk about the following:

*   Any confusing parts
*   Any unknown words
*   Text to text, text to self, text to world connections
*   The main idea in each chapter or heading

Encourage children to use context clues to determine the meaning of any unknown words. These strategies will help children learn to analyze the text more thoroughly as they read.

When you are finished reading this book, turn to the next-to-last page for **After-Reading Questions** and an **Activity**.

TABLE OF CONTENTS

ALL ROADS LEAD TO THE ARTS

Your interests can start you on the path to a job you will love. Are you passionate about the arts? Do you enjoy being creative? A career in the studio may be just right for you! Let's explore different career paths that all lead to a life of creativity.

Keep an eye out for these icons to learn more about how to achieve your goals:

Minimum education/training required

Average time commitment (beyond a high school diploma or GED)

Ways to boost your qualifications

LYRICIST

Lyricists write the words to all kinds of songs. Whether they're writing the lyrics for a catchy jingle, a musical, or a huge pop hit, lyricists spend lots of time in music studios. They may **collaborate** with composers, who are able to write the music, to make a complete song. Lyricists can work as **freelancers** and work for more than one client at a time. They can also work full-time as staff writers for music publishers or media agencies.

collaborate (kuh-LAB-uh-rate): work together to do something

freelancers (FREE-lans-uhrs): people who get paid for each individual job they do

GED or high school diploma

No set time

Learn to write music
Bachelor's degree

RECORDING ENGINEER

Recording engineers are in charge of capturing live sounds in a recording studio. They can record anything from voice-overs for animated films to an orchestra's debut album. Their jobs include setting up equipment, instruments, and the computer programs used to record. Recording engineers may also work with artists on perfecting their sound before recording. Then, they edit, mix, and master the recording to make it sound better.

 GED or high school diploma

 No set time

 Audio engineering **apprenticeship** program
Bachelor's degree in audio engineering

apprenticeship
(uh-PREN-tis-ship):
a job where someone
learns a skill by working
with an expert

CHOREOGRAPHER

The ones with all the moves! Choreographers create and design dances. Some perform their own work, but many teach their moves to other dancers to perform. Choreographers usually work with a particular dance style but can mix and match.

🎓 GED or high school diploma

🕐 Nothing set in stone

➕ Attend dance training programs after school and in the summer

Associate's, bachelor's, or master's degree in dance

Choreographers can work in many different settings. Some work for dance schools or professional performance companies. Others may work in the entertainment **industry**, choreographing routines for music videos, commercials, or films. A few may have their work featured in interactive dance video games!

industry (IN-duh-stree): a single branch of business or trade

Hints & Hacks

Get a head start and choreograph dances for school theater productions.

FASHION FORWARD

FASHION DESIGNER

Time to get dressed. Fashion designers create clothes, accessories, and shoes. They might use sketch pads or computer software to sketch out their design ideas. Their outfits can be seen anywhere from a high fashion runway show to the racks of a popular clothing store. Most designers create clothes for people, but some even design looks for animals!

 Bachelor's degree (required for most positions)

4 years

 Create a **portfolio**
Fashion design apprenticeship program

portfolio
(PORT-foh-lee-oh):
a collection of
drawings, paintings,
or photographs
presented together
in a folder

PHOTOGRAPHER

Say cheese! Photographers use their skills to capture images. They can work in private, fashion, and production studios taking pictures. They also need lighting and editing skills to get things picture-perfect. Most work as freelancers, but some can be hired full-time for businesses such as film companies or magazines. Depending on the **gig**, they may snap shots of movie scenes, models, or even meatballs!

No set requirements

No set time

Work as an assistant to a photographer
Associate's or bachelor's degree in photography

gig (gig): a temporary job

MAKEUP ARTIST

Makeup artists use cosmetic products to change or enhance how someone looks. They can work as freelancers or be employed by a company. There are also different industry options for makeup artists, such as fashion and entertainment. The skills they need vary depending on the industry and job assignment.

 No set requirements

 No set time

Offer free makeup services to aspiring models for photoshoots
Create a portfolio
Certification or associate's degree in cosmetology

In the world of fashion, a makeup artist may highlight a model's eyes for a photoshoot. For theater, a makeup artist may have to enhance a performer's features so they can be seen from the back row. In the film and movie industry, artists may have to transform a person's face into an alien!

Hints & Hacks

Show your skills online. Create makeup tutorial videos and share them on social media!

GAFFER

Light the way! A gaffer is an electrician who is in charge of the lighting in movie and television production studios. Their job starts by getting to know the project script. Then, they figure out what lights are needed and how they should be set up to shoot a scene. Gaffers collaborate with directors, producers, and their lighting team to get the job done.

GED or high school diploma

 No set time

Work as a lighting production assistant
Electrician training or apprenticeship program
Bachelor's degree

3D ANIMATOR

3D animators create moving images with depth. They can work in the film industry, they can animate video games, or they could work in graphic design for websites or advertising companies. Working with computer programs to create the animations is an important skill for these animators. Whether working on a blockbuster animated movie or the latest video game, these artists create beautiful images that bring stories to life.

Bachelor's degree (for most positions)

4 years

Create a portfolio
3D animator apprenticeship program

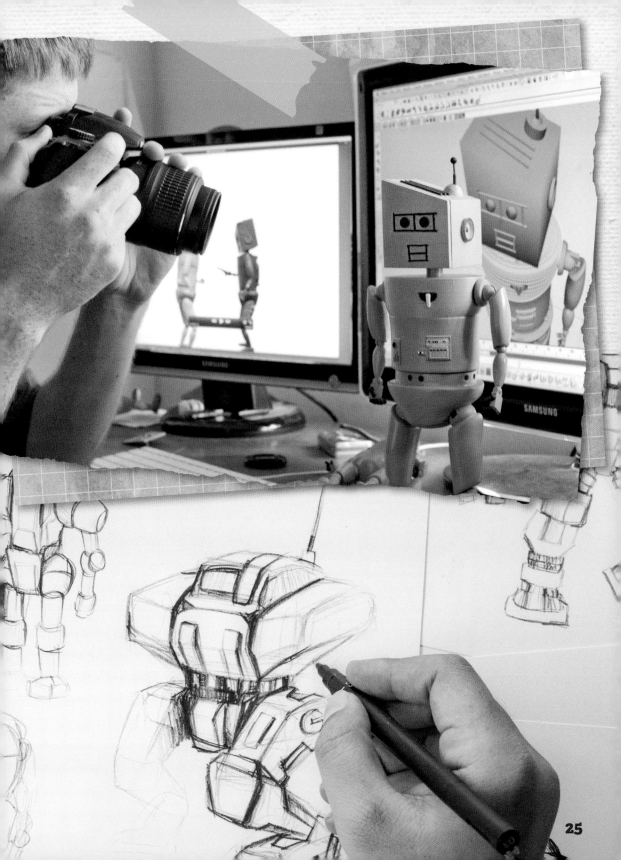

SET DESIGNER

A set designer creates the scenery and props for movie, TV, or theater productions. Estimating how much everything will cost is also part of their job. They study the project script before creating floor plans, sketches, and mini models of the set. Then set designers collaborate with a team to build and place their creations.

GED or high school diploma

No set time

Work as a set builder
Bachelor's degree

Set designers spend a lot of time recreating actual locations inside of a production studio. This can mean building what looks like the inside of a classroom or the top of the Statue of Liberty. Some are more comfortable bringing imaginary places to life, like a vampire's lair or a park full of dinosaurs!

Hints & Hacks

Take a technical drawing class in high school to learn how to make floor plans and models.

Look at the pictures. What do you remember reading on the pages where each image appeared?

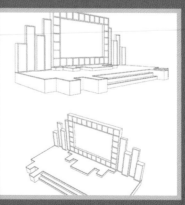

INDEX

AFTER—READING QUESTIONS

1. Which professional would you call to make you look like an alien?

2. Who is in charge of lighting?

3. What does a recording engineer do?

4. What qualifications would you want to have to be a 3D animator?

5. Whose work could you see in your local boutique?

ACTIVITY

Choose your favorite career from this title. Research the range of different types of positions this career can have. What differences do you see in the jobs? Is there a big difference in the amount of money you could make in this career? See if you can find out why.

ABOUT THE AUTHOR

Shantel Gobin loves helping people grow and achieve their goals. She enjoys writing to inspire new ways of thinking. It is her goal to create a generation of lifelong learners. She lives in Brooklyn, New York, where she works as a school psychologist and author.

www.rourkebooks.com

PHOTO CREDITS: cover, title page, TOC, pages 4-32: ©Charday Penn/ Getty Images; cover, title page, pages 8-9, 14-15, 18-19: ©marekuliasz/ Shutterstock.com; cover, title page: ©wundervisuals/ Getty Images, ©Olena Hromova/ Shutterstock.com, ©AS photostudio/ Shutterstock.com; Back Cover: ©Olya Fedorova/ Shutterstock.com, ©gdvcom/ Shutterstock.com; title page, TOC, pages 4-32: ©Moolkum/ Shutterstock.com; title page, pages 4-8, 10-14, 16, 18, 20-28, 30: ©Flas100/ Shutterstock.com; TOC, pages 4, 6, 14, 22, 30-32: ©My Life Graphic/ Shutterstock.com; pages 4, 7, 8, 10, 14, 16, 18, 23, 24, 27: ©13ree.design/ Shutterstock.com; pages 4-5, 7-12, 14-16, 18, 21, 24, 27, 29: ©MichaelJayBerlin/ Shutterstock.com; pages 7, 23: ©Realstockvector/ Shutterstock.com; pages 5, 7, 9, 11, 12, 17, 19, 22, 25, 29: ©Rawpixel.com/ Shutterstock.com; pages 4, 7, 8, 10, 14, 16, 18, 23, 24, 27: ©SweetRenie/ Shutterstock.com; page 5: ©DedMityay/ Shutterstock.com, ©tdub303/ Getty Images, ©YakobchukOlena/ Getty Images, ©Rawpixel/ Getty Images; page 7: ©miodrag ignjatovic/ Getty Images, ©millann/ Getty Images; pages 8-9: ©gorodenkoff/ Getty Images; page 9: ©banjongseal324/ Getty Images; pages 9, 30: ©shironosov/ Getty Images; page 10: ©mhatzapa/ Shutterstock.com; page 11: ©SFROLOV/ Shutterstock.com; pages 11, 30: ©wundervisuals/ Getty Images; page 12: ©SFROLOV/ Shutterstock.com; page 14: ©Vyacheslav Prokofyev/ZUMAPRESS/Newscom; pages 14-15: ©JGalione/ Getty Images; page 15: ©UfaBizPhoto/ Shutterstock.com, ©Anna Ismagilova/ Shutterstock.com; pages 16-17: ©Gorodenkoff/ Shutterstock.com; pages 17, 30: ©shironosov/ Getty Images; pages 18-19: ©AnnaTamila/ Shutterstock.com; page 19: ©Benjamin Askinas/ZUMA Press/Newscom; page 20: ©Stephen Chung/ZUMA Press/Newscom; pages 21, 30: ©Ihor Bulyhin/ Getty Images; page 21: ©Jair Cabrera Torres/dpa/picture-alliance/Newscom; page 22: ©Grusho Anna/ Shutterstock.com; pages 22-23: ©guruXOOX/ Getty Images; pages 24-25: ©Chaosamran_Studio/ Getty Images; pages 25, 30: ©Joshua Sudock./ZUMApress/Newscom; page 26: Gallica/the Bibliothéque Nationale de France/ Wikimedia Commons; page 27: ©Pavel L Photo and Video/ Shutterstock.com; pages 28-29: ©Idealphotographer/ Shutterstock.com; page 29: ©tele52/ Shutterstock.com; pages 29-30: ©Rusli/ Shutterstock. com;

Edited by: Hailey Scragg
Cover and interior design by: Alison Tracey

Library of Congress PCN Data

Careers in the Studio / Shantel Gobin
(Design Your Future)
ISBN 978-1-73165-286-7 (hard cover)
ISBN 978-1-73165-256-0 (soft cover)
ISBN 978-1-73165-316-1 (e-book)
ISBN 978-1-73165-346-8 (e-pub)
Library of Congress Control Number: 2021952170

Rourke Educational Media
Printed in the United States of America
01-2412211937